WELCOME TO THE EXCITING BEAUTIFUL CHRISTMAS JE

Everything you need to make a festive pin is included with this book. You can make the other pieces of jewelry in this book with some easy-to-find materials. When you go outside, keep your eyes open for small natural objects that are pretty and Christmassy—pine cones, dried flowers, twigs and branches, and sprigs of holly and pine. At a craft or variety store, stock up on seed beads, barrel beads, sequins, tiny Christmas bells and balls, artificial flowers, holiday fabric, tinsel pipe cleaners, glitter paint, and gold cord. Recycle: use beads and earring hooks from old jewelry, last year's Christmas cards, shirt boxes, wrapping paper, tissue paper, ribbon, and elastic cord from gift packages. Look in the sewing basket for needles and thread, safety pins, and scraps of pretty fabric.

You'll have fun making and wearing your beautiful Christmas jewelry. And handmade pins, hair ornaments, bracelets, and necklaces make wonderful holiday gifts for family and friends.

Hints:

- Gather all the materials you will need for each project before you begin.
- Many of these jewelry pieces can be made into Christmas ornaments. Instead of attaching safety pins or earring hooks to the pieces, use ornament hooks and hang your "jewelry ornaments" on your tree! Ornaments make great gifts, too!
- Experiment with different designs. Add beads, sequins, small bells, or other materials for a one-of-a-kind look.

FESTIVE FRINGED BOW

Materials Needed

- 4-inch x 4-inch (10 cm x 10 cm) square of green felt
- 4-inch x 4-inch (10 cm x 10 cm) square of red felt
- scissors
- 14-inch (36 cm) length of red ribbon, 1/8 inch (.3 cm) wide
- 24-inch (60 cm) length of white lace, 1/2 inch (1 cm) wide
- 12-inch (30 cm) length of green, red, and gold braid
- small gold bell
- safety pin or ponytail loop
- glue (optional)

Get into the holiday spirit! Everything you need to make this delightful Christmas bow comes with this book. All you add are scissors, a safety pin or ponytail loop, and your imagination!

1. Snip along two opposite edges of both pieces of felt. Make cuts no more than 3/4-inch (2 cm) deep and about 1/4-inch (.6 cm) apart.

2. Fold the piece of green felt like an accordion. The folds should run in the same direction as the fringe.

3. Pinch together the center of the green felt and wrap the red ribbon around it. Knot the ribbon to hold it in place, but don't cut it.

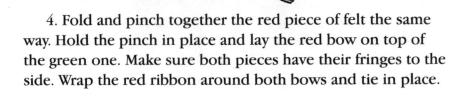

4. Fold and pinch together the red piece of felt the same way. Hold the pinch in place and lay the red bow on top of the green one. Make sure both pieces have their fringes to the side. Wrap the red ribbon around both bows and tie in place.

5. Make four bow-like loops in the lace. Hold the lace so there are two loops and one end on each side. Place the lace on top of the red felt.

6. Make two bow-like loops with the braid and position on top of the lace. Hold in place while you bring the ends of ribbon around. Wrap the four bows together and tie a single knot.

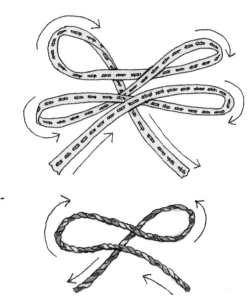

7. String the bell on the ribbon. Slide it to the center of the bow and tie a single knot. Wrap the ribbon around to the back and tie a double knot. The ends of the ribbon should hang down approximately 3 inches (8 cm).

8. When the bow is finished, slip the head of an open safety pin through the knot on the back so you can wear it. Or string the ribbon through a ponytail loop and wear the bow in your hair.

CANDY WREATH PIN

Materials Needed

- 4-inch x 4-inch (10 cm x 10 cm) square of dark green felt
- 4-inch x 4-inch (10 cm x 10 cm) square of lightweight cardboard
- glue
- pencil
- sheet of tracing paper
- scissors
- jelly beans or other colorful candy
- 12-inch (31 cm) length of red ribbon, 3/4 inch (2 cm) wide
- safety pin

Here's a pin that's good enough to eat! And pretty enough to wear on a favorite sweater. Or pin it to your coat when you go caroling.

1. Glue the green felt to the cardboard and let it dry.

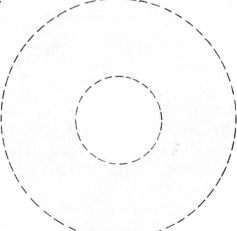

2. Trace the circle pattern onto tracing paper, and copy the pattern onto the back of the cardboard. Cut the circle and its center out.

3. Glue jelly beans or other candy onto your wreath. Or you can use buttons, sequins, dried flowers, shells, or painted macaroni for different looks.

4. Wrap the ribbon around your wreath and tie into a bow.

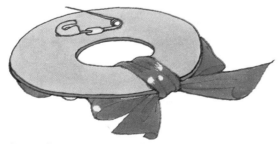

5. Open the safety pin and glue or tape it to the back of the wreath.

Hint:

- Leave the inner circle of cardboard uncut. Glue a picture of yourself or someone else in the center of the wreath.

VICTORIAN CHRISTMAS HEART

Materials Needed

- sheet of tracing paper
- sheet of lightweight cardboard
- scissors
- 8-inch x 8-inch (20 cm x 20 cm) square of soft sheer fabric, such as silk, light cotton, nylon, or luster fabric
- a small amount of polyfill or cotton
- needle and strong thread to match fabric
- sequins, beads, ribbons, and flowers to sew or glue to the heart.
- safety pin, ponytail loop, or ornament hanger

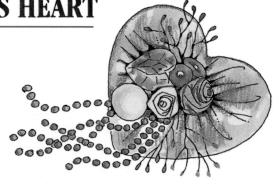

Have an old-fashioned Christmas! Make the heart exactly as it's shown here or experiment with your own ideas. You can even hang this heart on your Christmas tree.

1. Trace the heart pattern onto tracing paper. Transfer the pattern to the lightweight cardboard and cut out.

2. Place the cardboard heart in the center of the fabric square. Top with polyfill or cotton to make a puff.

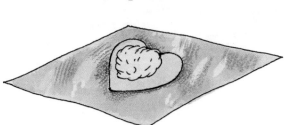

3. Gather the fabric up and around the heart and puff, bunching the fabric together in the center. Make sure the folds around the edges and at the center of the heart are neat

and smooth. Wind the thread tightly around the neck of the gathered fabric 5 or 6 times.

4. Double knot the thread. Trim away excess fabric, leaving only a short stump of material.

5. To make the fabric follow the top edge of the heart smoothly, use a needle and thread to make several stitches at the "v" between the curves of the heart. The stitches should pull the fabric down and back so that you get a perfect heart shape.

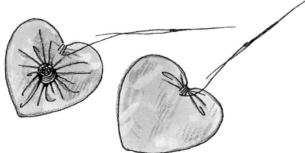

6. Sew or glue tiny beads, sequins, ribbons, and flowers around the stump. Sew a safety pin to the back to make a pin or add a ponytail loop or ornament hanger.

SHOOTING STAR NECKLACE

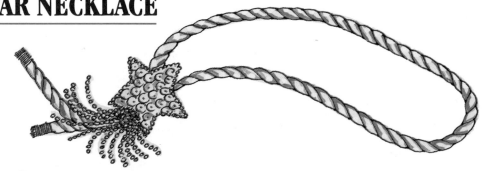

Materials Needed

- 32-inch (81 cm) length of gold metallic twisted cord
- transparent tape
- gold or yellow thread
- scissors
- glue
- gold sequined and beaded star, 2 1/2 inches (6 cm) wide
- 4-inch x 4-inch (10 cm x 10 cm) square of gold metallic or shiny yellow fabric
- 4-inch (10 cm) length of yellow satin ribbon, 1/8 inch (.3 cm) or 1/4 inch (.6 cm) wide

Slide the star up to your neck for a choker effect. Or let it hang down like a pendant. Or wear the star anywhere in between! No matter how you wear it, you'll shine.

1. Tape both ends of the cord to prevent fraying while you work. Starting above the tape, wrap gold or yellow thread very tightly around 1/4 inch (.6 cm) of each end of the cord. Cut the thread and glue the cut ends to the wrapped thread. Cut any remaining thread away.

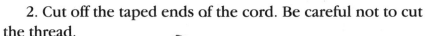

2. Cut off the taped ends of the cord. Be careful not to cut the thread.

3. Glue the fabric square to the back of the star, being careful to glue close to the edges of the star. Trim away excess material.

4. Glue or sew 2 small loops of yellow satin ribbon to the back of the star. Cut the ribbon to the right size. The loops should be small enough to keep the cord from falling out but big enough to let the star slide up and down.

5. Slide the two ends of the cord into the loops. Slip the necklace over your head and gently pull both ends of the cord to move the star up or down.

SHOE POM-POMS

Materials Needed

- 2 strips of red tulle, 2 1/2 inches (6 cm) wide and 36 inches (91 cm) long
- needle and red thread
- 2 red ribbon rosettes
- 8 red 20 mm bangles
- 8 clear-faceted beads
- glue
- sheet of tracing paper
- cardboard
- scissors
- 5-inch x 5-inch (13 cm x 13 cm) square of red felt
- 2 pieces of sticky backed Velcro tape, or a barrette or ponytail loop

Give your shoes some holiday pizazz! Or attach a pom-pom to a special Christmas gift!

1. Fold one piece of tulle in half lengthwise. Thread the needle with a double length of red thread. Knot the end. Sew half-inch (1 cm) stitches along the full length of the cut edges of the tulle. Make sure the stitches don't cross over the edge of the tulle.

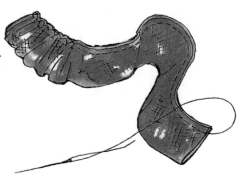

2. Check that the knot in the thread is secure, then pull the thread through the tulle to make gathers. Continue to pull until you have tight little gathers and the strip starts to curl into a circle.

3. With the needle and thread still attached, place a ribbon rosette in the center of the tulle circle. Wrap the tulle and

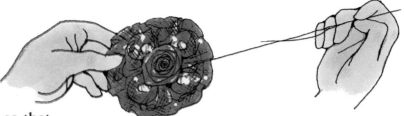

thread around the rosette, so that the tulle forms 2 layers around the rosette. Pull the thread until the gathered tulle fits snugly around the rosette's base.

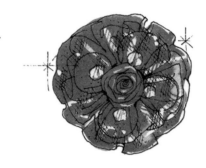

   4. Stitch the rosette to the gathered tulle. Secure with a double knot.

   5. Repeat steps 1-4 to make the other pom-pom.

   6. Sew 4 bangles to each pom-pom between the 2 rows of gathers. Sew or glue a bead on top of each bangle.

   7. Trace the circle pattern onto tracing paper. Transfer the shape to the cardboard and cut out. Use the cardboard pattern to cut two circles from the square of felt. Glue or sew each pom-pom to a circle of felt.

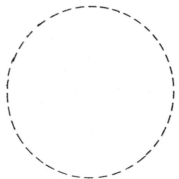

   8. If it is okay with your parents, peel the backing off the Velcro and attach the pom-poms to your shoes. Or glue to a barrette or ponytail loop for a hair decoration.

HOLIDAY PICTURE PIN

Materials Needed

- recycled Christmas card with a small, colorful picture
- scissors
- sheet of lightweight cardboard or heavy paper
- glue
- white pom-pom (optional)
- 4 or 5 small twigs, each about 4–6 inches (10 cm–15 cm) long. Try to find nice straight ones.
- strong thread—gold, red, green, or black
- 10 1/2-inch (27 cm) length of red or green ribbon, 1/8 inch (.3 cm) wide
- small bell—gold, red, or green
- safety pin
- gold sequin strip (optional)

This colorful Christmas pin gets a country look from a twig frame.

1. The picture you choose should be a square or a rectangle with four straight sides, none longer than the twigs. Cut out the picture. Cut cardboard the same size and glue the picture to it. If you want, glue the pom-pom onto your picture for extra decoration.

2. Break or cut twigs to the same length as the sides of your picture. Lay the twigs over and under one another, as shown. Glue the four corners together.

3. When the glue dries, wrap the corners with thread to give a rustic look. (See picture.) Starting at the top left-hand corner of the frame, wrap the thread five times from the inside corner of the frame to the angle made by the ends of

the twigs. Then wrap the thread around the remaining two outside angles. Wrap the inside corner another five times and then the outside angles, to make an "X" pattern. Repeat for the rest of the corners. Cut the thread and glue to the backs of the twigs.

4. String the ribbon through the bell and around the bottom twig. Tie a bow.

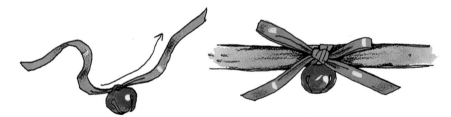

5. Glue the twig frame to the front of the picture. Glue the pin to the back.

Hint:

- To make a free-standing picture frame, glue one end of a twig to the back of the frame at an angle. The free end of the twig should be even with the bottom of the frame. Or, to make a tree ornament, glue the ends of the gold sequin strip to the back and hang on the tree.

13

MERRY CHRISTMAS STRETCH BRACELET

Materials Needed

- 36 barrel beads, 18 red, 18 white
- 36 inches (91 cm) of elastic gold cord

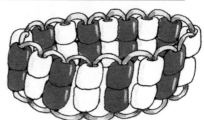

This bracelet makes a great gift because it stretches to fit any size wrist.

1. String 2 red beads onto the cord. Slide them to the middle of the cord.

2. String 2 white beads on one end of the cord. Pass the other end of the cord through the beads in the opposite direction.

3. Pull both ends of the cord evenly until the white beads rest on top of the red ones. Make sure both ends of the cord are still the same length.

4. Repeat steps 2 and 3 to string the rest of the beads.

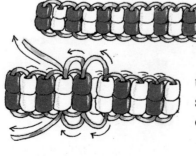

5. Work the extra cord back through the beads you've already strung to secure the ends within the other beads.

14

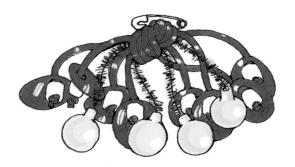

BANGLE DANGLE PIN

Materials Needed

- 40-inch (100 cm) length of red satin rat-tail cord
- 18-inch (46 cm) length of gold cord
- scissors
- 8 white barrel beads
- 8 red bangles
- 4 miniature gold Christmas balls
- safety pin

Dangling bangles and shiny Christmas balls are sure to get you into the holiday spirit.

1. Cut the red rat-tail cord into 4 equal pieces. Cut the gold cord in half.

2. Knot the end of one piece of red rat-tail cord. Slip on 1 white bead, 2 red bangles, and another white bead. Knot the other end of the cord. Slide one bead and one bangle to each end of the cord.

3. Repeat for the three other red rat-tail cords.

4. Tie a miniature gold ball to both ends of each gold cord.

5. Hold the 4 red rat-tail cords in your hand. Drape the gold cords over them.

6. Tie the 4 red rat-tail cords into a simple knot. Slip the safety pin through the knot in the cords to wear as a pin. Or sew on a ponytail loop and use as a hair ornament.

SILVER BELL EARRINGS

Materials Needed

- silver tinsel pipe cleaner, 11 inches (28 cm) long
- pencil
- 2 small silver bells
- scissors
- 14 inches (36 cm) red ribbon, 1/8-inch (.3 cm) wide
- pair of silver earring hooks

Jingle through the holidays! When silver bells ring, Christmas is on the way.

1. Cut the pipe cleaner in half. Wrap one half around the pencil. Slip it off with the twist in place.

2. Slip one end of the twisted pipe cleaner through the loop on the bell. Bend the pipe cleaner back to hold it securely.

3. Cut the ribbon in half. Tie one piece of ribbon in a bow just above the bell.

4. Slip the other end of the pipe cleaner through the eye of the earring hook, and bend back to fasten.

5. Repeat to make the second earring.

HINT:

- Earring hooks are sold in most jewelry stores.